GRETA BELLAMACINA

WHO WILL MAKE
THE FIRE

This first edition 2024 published by Cheerio Publishing
in association with New River Press

www.cheeriopublishing.com
info@cheeriopublishing.com

www.thenewriverpress.com

Printed and bound in Great Britain by TJ Books

Typeset in Mrs Eaves by Robert Montgomery

The Mrs Eaves font was designed by Zuzana Licko for Emigre
in 1996. It is an adapation of the Baskerville font and named after
John Baskerville's wife, Sarah Eaves, who worked with Baskerville
on the design of his fonts but was not given credit in her lifetime.

cover photograph by Melanie Rodriguez
author photos Tom Craig and Oliver Hadlee Pearch

A CIP catalogue record for this book is available from the British Library.

ISBN 978-1-7394405-9-6

This book is dedicated to

Robert Montgomery
Niall McDevitt
Michael Horovitz
Riccardo Vannuccini

CONTENTS

I wrote that the beauty was a place to dream,
so I collected the paintings for the books,
and, the books started to collect the roses.

Greta Bellamacina

WHO WILL MAKE THE FIRE

To live, to really live in the scaffoldings of a cathedral,
to live in this world filled with hawk wings
hands deep in a basket of fruit,
to get lost like a rock,
to bite into the poison
the sunlight in the apple,
the blooded flowers in the apple.

To live in the chasing charge of the light,
to live and to not have to survive,
to burn again and again and then sleep,
to let death give birth like the sea,
the sea an eternal child
tangled in a deep well of rainwater.

To hold on with strange pain
the godless myth of it all
to dream of yesterday,
to pass on the wood,
the upstanding bits left after the storm.

To live between the sky and the earth,
to walk on mama's earth and put your hands on the wind

to call the wind a friend blowing its disguise like a
                                        shadow horse,
to have a bit of mind caught up in it.

To watch this orchestra of madness fill you with a sort of
                                        manic satisfaction,
to watch you slowly go bit by bit,
to watch all of the greats live in you and then die in you
                                        their voices,

their wicked, wicked ways

building you up and destroying you like that.

To never truly know the love of a loved one,
to give everything to the person above and below you,
to follow the tree's white arrows,
criss-crossed
           peace
                cross-crissed,
to live in the pale eyes of the moon
an animal that hunts starlight.

To live in the blue wind,
to live in the blue wind trap,
to outlive the priest carrying holy water,
to live in the cold,
to ask, who will make the fire?

THE TREES MOVE DEEPER UNDERGROUND

There are plants that live better in the valley drought
than in the rain,

the bees are gentle until wrestled,

underneath the earth there is a wishing well that is
waiting to be found, living in the soiling prayers of dew.

The trees move deeper underground, a digging tribesman
searching for an underworld to rest his bones.

Alive and breathing like a forest
we wake up again and again,

the stone column gives out time,
its shadows are ariels bible-ing the floor, darting unloose.

Behind the iron gates
the horses remain in the fields,
braver than a shudder,
lamplighting the floor with their infinity.

The children live in a mythical world far away from here
putting out the fires and saving the paper,
they know things we do not know,
they are sadder than us and more broken
they pour with light, immortalising mosaic wind
entranceways.

The castle is empty
the furniture is stolen,
the wasteland waits on the bed of questions

it points from all sides, asking

can you hear me...
helloooooooO

The weather is searching,
no-one and nothing answers back.

the wasteland remains rhetorical...

From time to time, the moon shows both sides,
moon in blackness /moon in whiteness.
Two shaded eyes.

The windows are the waterlines to the city.
The people inside of them are shipwrecked,
they call it a home, but it is a long way from the beginning.
Something in their hearts is unmatched in their eyes,
longing never leaves you when home is a feeling.

The soul is a fox,
it roams the cities at night for someone to love, for
someone to let in.
Shadeless, dragging its great mouth,
teeth out.

The morning remains the anchor to the day
a kind of heaven walking away from itself.
The evening is what gives the morning its rage,
its new cold blue insolent joy against death.

Still, newborn loneliness hangs on every corner.

OUR WOE SOUNDS LIKE LOVE

Come grow into the devastating darkness
into our sleepless sun,

firehouse umbrella.

The loneliest star is calved at the alter
into the light of the rocking blessing-song.

Our woe sounds like love
hardening our ghosts

changing the nevers.

I take it to bed each night, correcting the punctuation of
its arrow

wrapping it like a present that hangs around my neck,
a drenching sob, fruit stone.

This is the last day of my life
love lies bleeding.

I watch the flowers grow like good needles
holding the earth inwards.

Singular instruments recording the air
silent faces,

the rain rivers in their mouths
drowning seeds.

ENDING SUNFLOWERS

The treaty of the sunflowers is walking and closing
agreeing to give up the world for the solace of breath.
Breaking their picture frames lashed yellow eyes,
agreeing to the modesty and the boredom of the wild
                                        rain—
slowly dawning to dawning, a little red tear,
the sun turns away and the little fires go out.

HAULING A PAIR OF PITCH BLACK WINGS

We broke our hearts on the same day so we could find
each other,
a shy house with a broken sea at its door.

Bodiless, I dive into your arms
the bees carry their candles
each one lit from honey, star-like feathers.

Leftover flowers sit in water that are asking who?
Unrested hand prints with a clicking blood clock.

Downstairs the supermarket is dancing,
glittering cold. Winter intestines fly

no memory until now.
The room is a God who is rowing and sallowing a blade.
Knuckles that are motherly rocks,
that are saying and unsaid.

The bed, a fascinating stone
does not stop writing the sky above it.
A long summary of dismantled goodbyes and Mondays,
each one carrying a nativity of your love

a clay Mary and a lamb
hauling a pair of pitch black wings.

WINTER CAME WITH A DEVOURING
CIGARETTE TREE

Winter came with a devouring cigarette tree.
In it London burnt, an extravagant horse riding into
the sun—

The fruit stole a piece of the fog from the vegetables
their faces grew backwards weeping into the flowers
downwards into the earth.

Nine lives of lost company wintering an allotment of
                                          surrender,
trailing an unlisted blue death,
Sinead O'Connor digs an empty hole in the garden.

Ash undoes earth
rubbled cloth and a pile of empty gloves
I dressed myself in their stares—
straight into the lost property of the rich,
confetti washed leaves unwanted.

I keep the light left on,
invisible tree and a somewhere room.

The lone pig stayed for a while trying to prove its wisdom

to the howling mud.

ELECTRIC TREE

It's Christmas Day and you're holding my hand in the
                                 empty road
all of our dreams are wrapped away now.
God has gone back to the sea,
the waves are crashing somewhere
pain is big out there, so big I forget to feel it.

The gulls leave pre-dawn
our house is still asleep.

There is a melody in the suspended clock
one hand to the ground, the other one with its palm out
holds a broken flower.

We reach the electric tree,
everything is brown but the red hair of the tree.
I remember thinking that it looked like happiness
                                       last winter
long locks alight with red happiness over this earth,
an upwards rain fire at our feet.

THE MILE LONG HOUSE IN YOUR RECOVERY

The mile long house in your recovery is filled with holes,
the wind is silent in it.

All of the gods live and die in it,
the god of the everyday church is here.

The birds fly in with hallucinations of the moon,
so bright the sunshine casts a mood-ocean.

Some of the rooms are laughing spiderwebs,
speechless unable to require a language for life.

The wind returns flipped in a collapsed hood—
a thousand tiny daggers at the windows,

a thousand tiny daggers taken from the ground with
memory loss,
a poor diamond in bits— maybe the first poor diamond.

A malingering of sad desire,
you feel every single dig like a joke erupting in a bullring.

You go out hunting for the poor diamond anyway,
some of the rooms are worse that others,
some have done their best.

In another room there is a nurse on her knees counting
                                   the melting stars
the wind has become separated from the sky here,
the sky is unable to keep warm.

The superstition of the stars hang onto the chairs,
and all the people in them become panicked.

In every corner there is the dust of the things that get left
                                        behind—
a stone girl with an angelic uncollected dream,

lavender above the bed for calm
a pitch-black ballet with Pina Bausch eyes shut.

The wind that is always a miraculous horse,
presses its face to the wall.

The horse can be in the house for days,
it remains mythical because it takes just what it needs.

The wind has the last place and the first place in its
                                        direction,
the door remains firmly bolted.

Sometimes this realisation keeps you smiling,
sometimes this realisation pushes you further away.

DOGWOMAN

I wonder how many women I have to be in this body
                                        of a dog
mouth open wide
a well of gathered rain water
slowly turning the stone blue.
A twelve month grave of empty crystal glasses
teeth holding the steps of a muddy field
an assembly of white cloud hammers.

LOOK HERE COMES A MOUNTAIN

Pain takes the flowers back,
small heads of enveloping tombs
go inwards.

Salvaged devotions
hang on deeper than a claw.
Look here comes a mountain.

SEND THE FLOWERS BACK INTO THE EARTH

Someone here said you had to be crazy to
send the flowers back into the earth
exalted beggars sinking the fall
some quicker, all followers.
Holy tongued non-profits
skulls of wilderness in the headlights.

I will meet you there,
lowered
turning away from it all
I will hold the old coins out like a daffodil
pour my heart into every single one
protesting peace
making a pedestal of irregular light
pretending to gain time
until spring.

A MOMENT OF DAWN

Past and present sun is reduced to asleep wood in the
plane trees.

Permanence is an illusion that burns down the calendar
before you wake.
The mirrors are careful not to magnify the language
of time,

the hour is egoless,
a bird is mistaken for freedom.

The air sings—

we are the prisoners of miracles
we are the return of hope.
The insane lungs that keep up the sails
the drowned virgins of rapture
the farmers,
luminous heart stone inmates.

Bits of earth pyramid to it,
flowers crash and laugh in the absorption of the light

the garden has a secret circle sewn into it.
It lives in the hope of new life,
drowning in the selflessness of water.

Still death has to come a billion times in order for you to
believe it.
All belief is laid out like a beach of sun worshipers,
the grass is the first to hold up its hands to the dawn.

LAMER THAN LOVE
for Michael Horovitz

You described it like watching birth,
hands filled with frost,
a dozen birds inside your skin wing-stamping.

They looked and looked for you all night
but all they could find was a stack of books.
On the walk home you see an elephant's face on
                              Colville Terrace,
incandescent eyes of Blake dismantling the words in the
                                            air.

The words fall over you
an afterburst of smoked stillness,
some pop in silent etchings,
some remain high up in the carbon mass of stardust

some are already alight with the happy song,
ha ha hee ha ha hee
ink suns
waiting to be mailed out,
new departures.

Somewhere your bed awaits for you up a flight of stairs,
all your things cradling the years in a fairyland of
alphabets, with an invitation of rosemary red keeping
                                        its promise.

A painted Jazz sightline/// a lost office,
cold water windowscape.

No heaven without a heaven,
purple is the colour.

The clock set bright
the hour is on.

UNBOTHERED ABOUT BEING JESUS-LIKE

Greed speaks to the moon all night long

fishing out the stars with a slow clay chain
sweet lamp heads with their hearts pulled out.

Unbothered about being Jesus-like,
greed rides the sky moors.

Stable green, a tree funeral,
a rocky wall to a further field.

Earth birds land on the shores,
sea mammals leap for the land.

I've heard that the moon lives on the idea of being present
sometimes the news makes this impossible,
she temporarily dies.

Greed laughs anyway
blowing the horizon crescent
unbothered about having a spirit.

The emblem of sky is gossiped up wrong
wielded in and out of the walls

The trees outline soundless,
perfectly joined,
harmonious edges on a fever hurl.

The moon is the sea's promise
washing and chiming
a bell.

The free stay poor
growing a centurygarden of small miracles out of dried tea.

Greed says
go back down to where you came from with all your colours
it's spoiling everything

The flowers are confused because they didn't pick their colours
The colours are confused because they didn't write their poetry.

COVER THE ROAD WITH YOUR MOTHER'S THINGS
from the film 'Commedia'

Cover the road with your mother's things
blooded love letters to the trees.

Hips in the ground keeping the beggar moth dreaming
growing into the masculine lines of autumn,
the feminine lines of jasmine bending
into the arc of the flowers bowing.

A hundred war flags subtracting the angelhood-lands
breathing into the lungs of a new world.

I DO NOT HATE MY ENEMY
for Niall McDevitt

I will plant a field of trees,
identical sunlamps with child-woman-boy eyes
they will blink into the fog with the last openness of the
                                            moon.

I will burn with my book of soil there
lighter and lighter
harvesting the body that holds onto me.

The tree to the tree:
I do not hate my enemy

—hush'd windsun travellers

the tree to the tree:
I do not hate my enemy

—believed earth halo
daylight heaven sleeping in poems.

THE WIND KEEPS ON

A countryside of levitation
blowing a heart made of rain.

The wind keeps on
a messenger of crossroads
an inaudible wand of hemispheres.

Flying embered light of future gold.

Flying embered light of dying wood.

A magic performance of unbibled tricks—
A cold morning.
The iron bird with blossom feathers.
The emerald fields in July.
Your small hand holding me like a gloved god.

The wind keeps on
a five mile ferris wheel voice singing :

big boys don't cry
　　　　　big boys don't cry.

OUR OWN FAITH CRUSHING THE SNOW INTO FLOWERS

We moved closer to the water,
    to the wintering nest that rolls as it crushes

to the second inn of imaginings,
    the open clouds set in the desolate and the
    unbelonged.

Fallen graves lamping the fields,
    the sticks on the ground struck by rain in a row of
strange celebration light.

the sun amuleting at our toes like a wild dog,
    living in modern hours that are shut up in the
    rituals of the sea.

The night boiling at the stove
    waiting for your lovely ways.

We moved closer to the skirling sorrow of our children,
    our own faith crushing the snow into flowers.

To the horses sharing the land,
    living with the birds, uncrowned speed
    testimonies.

The leaving ladybirds waiting on death,
    crawling through the small towns flicking a bat
    black Christmas/

a pharmacy in suburbia, built with the spirit of the palm
    trees,
    the abandoned garden of our dreams.

We moved closer to ourselves, slipping into characters
       driven by burning wood,
          closer to the pain, closer than caring like we've
       never cared before.

To America, Ginsberg's tears naked in the bricks,
       the trees lingering into our bones as we sleep in
       their wind.

The dark vague undertones of the road,
       a one hundred geometry lined fang.

To a metaphor of lightness resolving in and out of the
       lampshade of our small little lives.

MELTDOWN*

Smoke waltzes into war
speedwell-pink in its grip
the nightingale follows.

Forgiveness is rotten here,
the promised land burns a thousand candles

the saints swim back to shore
they hold out their hands to the wind
dropping bits of clothing one by one.

The stars have their backs turned this time
the sky is bare
this time is the last time

one by one it's all long gone—
the waltz kills the game.

Truth travels, it is written in the heart,
eventually the house lies down
some life you wished on,
goodnight.

Spring remains conscious underneath the ground
the seed has been sown,
rain in its mouth.

*written for and performed as part of the anti-war theatre piece "Angelus Novus" by ArteStudio at the Museo dell'Ara Pacis (the altar of peace) in Rome, 14th May 2022.

THE STAR ON YOUR HEAD

The star on your head is a child,

    triangle wings with a lake inside—

        arms long like the railings of an

            important garden.

IMAGINING THE MORNING YOU DIED

Breakfasting on the plug's arrest
the triangle is broken.
A single moment that might miracle you closer with the
weight of a dream.
A statue force coated in gold, holding an atom,
right handed to left handed—
a masonry stone woman on a bed of church stone
surrounded by 8 hanging saints,
joined together by just a string.

HEAVEN IS A REALITY UP IN THE SKY

The river is a trembling cow
war in its womb
an invisible spring.

A black and white butterfly
on this chess board of lined up strangers from some
other life.

The water loves in memories
years from now,
years back, days on days

water so fast staring into space
impossible mornings —
                                    but first we must find the flowers.

FROST

A falling ghost-halo hangs its wing

over the quiet machine of the tree.

EVEN THE WIND IS DEAD**

for Nadiya Sukhorukova

This city is fallen
its heart is an aerial bomb
the basements are filled with rain
no time to protest
the trees have all come down.
The calendar is erased.
The war has begun,
even the wind is dead.

**Commissioned for and performed at "An Evening For Ukraine's Refugees" charity fundraiser, Wednesday 30th March, 2022 at The Tabernacle, Notting Hill.*

GONE WIND

gone wind hell hole
gone back to the...

gone with your fingers in my womb
gone with your lodging mind

gone for second helpings
licking it all right back like that.

gone with your hunting chariot rider
gone wind bleeding from star light to star light.

gone with your wind tippy toeing locks
parting the tree sockets turning towards the sun like a
                                        pretend mother.

gone wind
exact hole punched, skyless

gone with your sacrifice.

gone with your fold up bed sleeping on my heart.

gone with your new directions

gone with your birdcage knotting a rushed collapse
de-bible-ing the birdsong

gone around unkind

noncommittal helium forest

gone with your awful stare
gone with your robber look

gone wind halved-bronzed tangle scum.

MY SWEET HOLLYHOCK

Adrift in pink you brought with it your heartache

heavy-headed

hurried to weeping

a laddered look

in all five eyes.

SNOW WHITE

Snow melted rain on grey diagonals

senating a secret world dance

a white bed of our silk history

half-remembering the fairytales of purity and the
morning with its secret sun.

LOW WIND

All tributes burnt madly to the ground,
loose illuminations.

The Pantheon sky where spring is a recurring dream,
a suspended halo

hovering, just to come down.
The end of the year again,

people ask me how I feel now,
being out of the city, but the city is in the trees
and the trees are louder than the listening albums
of unused paper.

WIND THROUGH THE TREES

A garment from god dressed in a rose,
blossoming as it speaks
all your good looks gone,
the piano, an alien resuscitation.

A drag from a sunshine junkie
unafraid of the bright light,
fingers deep in midway erections
dragging a white broken arrow between your teeth.

THEY LIVE IN THE CITIES BUT THEIR DREAMS ARE SHAKEN IN FIELDS OF BROKEN SEAS

for Lorca & Lucian

The children are small,
full of violins and stones that drop to the ground like
cannon chills.

They live in the cities,
but their dreams are shaken in fields of broken seas.

They live in the capital,
but their dreams are
               wild goats on the side of mountains.

BLUE WIND TRAP

There is a sonnet at the bottom of the sea, opening its
shell like a petrol bomb.

Occasionally wind stops
it drops everything in a motion clap, printing a
blue halation
an aquamarine tree.

Hands part to the ground like useless traps,
the great balloon inside of me, that is a womb, that is
ten women, pops.

Nobody is safe
life is a stranger to itself.

It is impossible to not let it get you down,
to let it fill the shut person in you,
the one who was once filled with precious abundance.

You have the same eyes that open and close in water
but on this day you are given a calendar of the sun that
is a star fighting its last bite.

Detached, there is a voice inside your head
writing up a contract full of stories and pictures,
it does not stick, it does not run away.

All the important sentences are lost.

A WEIGHTLESS PREGNANCY

Blue wind in the mind
a death mask does something inside,
twenty-two love poems lost.
Waterlilies for eyes.

A weightless pregnancy,
identical tremble-joy and tears—
a stewardess ribcage filled with fire and ash.

The doctor suggested I was depressed
and that every colour holds a metaphor for something,
the looking glass cradling an alphabet.

BLUE WIND IN THE LIGHT OF DAWN

Shooting star runs back to death,
a hundred slipped hours with the mind of a baby,
into the dying clouds of a black-lit house,
violently challenging sleep.

The blue wind obeys the light of dawn at this time,
the light of the dawn pretends not to notice,
egoless, all its spirits turn around and close up
into a knuckled flower //

The trees below with their cliff crossed antlers
                         point to the sun.
The trees are laughing and crying
the golden halo of the virgin moon keeps quiet.

The light of the dawn is the last thing to go,
the curtain leaves its window and the
window leaves its wall.

BREATHING IS THE PARTY

breathing is the main groove
breathing is the meeting
breathing is the party
breathing is the book
breathing is the club
breathing is the knife

THE DEVIL LOVES TO DANCE

This dance
a place to reach in the somewhere else,
the devil's cathedral is in the surrender of the missing,
knocking new light into the morning light.

On the street corner where two borders meet,
the church behind the wall sings all night
the street lamp stands to the side,
blowing shadows in time to its song
one is a lion, the other is a bird.

They keep their anthem into the night
two street lovers holding on to one another,

no promise is too deep,
no love is further than the night.

This dance is holy,
this dance is a husband and wife
tangled railings
trying to stay like this
touch by touch—
this place might *save us*.

We will meet again and publish our poems in soap,
the sunlight will run between the gaps,
stealing the hidden flower gardens inside the apples.

Moving to their slow decay
extraordinary lilies creak in.
At the kitchen table, the devil moves with the game
dancing on your show

tapping into the secret council of your heart,
the devil loves to dance.
No ordinary time waits for you like this
this dance is special, a hymn to the end,
a betrayer to the ghosts.

This dance, irregular grievance on the beating drum
lonesome violin
living on the front door of your heart.

The devil's door is covered in a thankless gold
lighting up the garden inside the tree,
inside the fruit.

Covered in darkness, but filled with the epoch of gold
holding up the confetti,
little bits of colourful paper you can buy in
the supermarket
to throw up and wait for them to come down.

OLIVE TREE

travelling Lazarus keeps on
someplace between birth and death
a crumble of abandonment
tinselling in a wind bath

urning out the water
urning out the index
speed sorrow— tada! resurrection—
joy in water.

DEFERRED EROSION

from 'Commedia' and inspired by Ingeborg Bachmann

The keeper of wind is not a weapon

The keeper of wind is not a wall of defence

The keeper of wind is not a house of dominance

The keeper of wind is not a politician of unloving
radiation

The keeper of wind is not one soul but a community of
wild flowers inhaling lost stones//

The keeper of wind is not an artillery thesaurus

The keeper of wind is not masculine, not male, not his

The keeper of wind is not a marvellous myth

The keeper of wind is not a body fighting for abundance

The keeper of the wind is not the resurrection of gold

The keeper of wind is not a blade of dismissive
namelands,

it is bigger and more deferred in its erosion

it is wider, lake-mouthed, feminine.

YELLOW WASTELAND SONG
for Lorca

Layout your things
put everything in a row
the colours are waiting for you,
say their names over again like a protection bride.

They say they do not understand me,
but they too are made from bits of silent gardens and
voices of baleful tears.

They say they do not understand me,
but they have been dancing in a chamber of sea-songs,
lilac blue infant of home.

Put the animals in a line so they are all facing out,
breathe in the small devout stare of things.

The wind that is writing in yellow at this time
is a perfectly balanced wasteland,
two colours holding a sunrise.

They say they cannot understand me,
but they are the makers of torchlight.

They say they cannot hear my calling,
but inside your eyes they hold the atmosphere of
                                         holy water,
blinking in the pounding collapse.

Why are all the people I love missing?

We once walked a long way in Zagreb to discover

a museum of broken hearts,
aisles of weather systems recorded,

a supermarket of things that make you weak
memories in the immediate, as you like
a gift you once gave holding the faith of a prophet.

Nothing escapes here
a searched dream sequence
nothing is wasted, all is precious and unthreatened
the sky shines for you here.

Blown here by the wind,
we will touch the glass together,
spit out the water onto the floor again and again
approach the rain like God.

Don't be afraid,
hold the puddles like magic and I will swim across
for you.

THIS PERSON INSIDE THE FLAME

Distant prayer rider
galleon bed of wall light
betrayer of the pen

ship hat coffin
mouth derailed in sun

Bunhill Fields campaigner
dancing the church window
expressions of brightness
death burning within death

Zimon in his room writing up his return
the angel of a blackbird keeping the lullabies to itself

cattle that are named cattle
blinking eyed cows
still named cattle
star and sun mankind

a long train journey with a quick lunch at the end of it
the explanation of dinosaurs
big and small nightmares
pigeons leap

the dragger of a great head
present failure
wind wings disturbing the trees
painless
daily plans
eternal interludes

the need for music with mad wishes
missing people

lines of toy animals ghosting the children

anthologised snowstorm
a tear crescent sky
a love that is dying

one more tree in the forest
talking fire whisper
one last castaway

sorrow chaining to memory
memory hailing melodies

this person inside the flame.

THIS HOUSE

You rest your wars in this house,
wild air rises like a friend
your bones have set sail many times
the moons with their seas have set into your heart—
into the orchestra of you here.

You wipe your blood and your failures onto the freshly
                                        painted floors,
hold onto the walls like an evening prayer
everything is here, you will not find it out there.

Two happy mice
we climb and climb into bed
a tray of medicine and milk bottles by our heads,

cloud testimonies
the broken windows we have yet to fix,
eyes replay the outside shapes and the cold white doves
                                        above,
fifty steps ahead of a dream.

You speak with the voice of Gary
before he died he spoke with a long distant laugh
telling you of the love he tried to keep,
if only he could keep it closer
if only he could tell the angels one last time
up to his attic held together with a disco ball gun and
a pair of fake teeth.

You rest your wars in this house,
there is a dust here held together with the legs of your
father walking towards a flame,

there is a dust here held together by wet wood
a sweet breeze in the smoke of our sons.

Nothing stays for long in this house but all is patient
the morning star is a god on our ceiling
you hold me like a rare world
travelling in darkness and ending in darkness
arriving in infinite light circles
to-night, to-morrow.

EARTH

I danced alone in the diagonals like a thief filling my
pockets, turning in the smoke of the candle

an unconceived heartbeat that is as slow as a river and
long as a river.

I shed all my children.

The wind in the radio remembers the trees
like a mother before she was a mother.

There is a handprint on my name
a dream endures the seasons
kindling a shivered face—

a haunted oakwood, with a return ticket.

EARTHLY CYCLES

She cools the windows of her eyes,
takes off her jewellery and puts it away in a box
in the ground,
a screwed door to a secret mind.

Undoing a 24 hour rotation of hurt-ling love,
a blow dry of tears
axis'ing melancholy, hugging breath.

Blue milk,
the smell of the wet sky somewhere shadows
straight talking rainwater, with a desire to forgive
that pours onto your shoes.

The apple is a factory cavern
devouring the floating legend of the morning.

She takes back the wood from the trees in ashes and
walks in bewilderment
her dress touches the sea.

Darkness empties into the angels
suffering something
that takes her to the skies.

LADYBIRD

I waited for the earth

the rain had the ghost of the future in its wings
the grain of the garden was inside of it
tapping through the night's piano.

The people I though I would be came in fright,
I was reduced to a looking flower
Petals like plates waiting to be served out.

Inside my throat held a well
rolling in quicksand
flapping through the night tracks of mice.

The birds keep flight
I bury my head in the trees.

Somewhere, there is a love that is further than us,
an unborn baby already named.

ILLUMINOUS WIND
a benediction

Illuminous wind in the light

illuminous wind in mercy-ial light

illuminous wind in the first cry of morning light

illuminous wind in the now time for peace light

illuminous wind sending a blessing light

illuminous wind in the gospel-stripping light

illuminous wind in the birds of fire light

illuminous wind in the fruit filled with black mass
                                                    star light

illuminous wind in the beheld light

illuminous wind in the salvation of beaten light

illuminous wind in the arms that birthed you in
                                                    threadbare light

illuminous wind in the bomb of torch light

illuminous wind blown in the manic faith of light

illuminous wind in ruby shoes walking on ultra-light

illuminous wind in decades of dream worship-light

illuminous wind in the immortal box light

illuminous wind at the blue throne of weeping light

illuminous wind moving in a shiver light

illuminous wind in the jagged unlanguaged light

illuminous wind called upon a dawn light,

I take you with me.

GLOSSARY

Greta occasionally invents new words in English, this is
a short glossary of the invented words in this book:

'Senating'— this is an invented verb. Perhaps the verb of the
noun 'senate', evoking the circular shape of The
Senate, and in this context of snow, evoking silent
judgement.

appears in SNOW WHITE, page 48.

'Mercy-ial'— an instinctive conflation of 'mercy' and 'mer-
curial'. In the context of 'mercy-ial light', as in the poem, it
is intended to infer that the light contains mercy, but is not
merciful.

appears in ILLUMINOUS WIND, page 70.

ACKNOWLEDGEMENTS

Thank you to—

Robert Montgomery, Clare Conville, Niall McDevitt,
Riccardo Vannuccini, Sylvia Whitman, Chris McCabe,
Heathcote Ruthven, Heathcote Williams, David Erdos,
Michael Horovitz, Zimon Drake, Jamie Lee the poet,
Kirsty Allison, Jacyln Bethany, Grace Cavanagh-Butler,
Natalie Hand, Brit Parks, Jennifer Francesca Sciuchetti,
Maria Sandrelli, Julie Goldsmith, Lucas Wetzel,
Juan José Vélez Otero, Maude Elms, Harriet Vyner,
Darren Biabowe Barnes, Maude Martel, Benny
Bellamacina, Lorca and Lucian Montgomery,
ArteStudio, The International Times, Shakespeare and
Company, The London Magazine, The National Poetry
Library.

photo: Tom Craig

ABOUT THE AUTHOR

Spearheading a new generation of female poets Greta Bellamacina writes with a liquid musicality and existential complexity. Influenced by the French Surrealist poets, Sylvia Plath and Anne Sexton, her work explores the themes of love, loss, nature, motherhood, depression, identity and war.

Greta read English at Kings College London and in 2014 she was short-listed as a Young Poet Laureate of London. Since then her poetry has gone on to be recognised internationally. The National Poetry Library commissioned three poems from Greta for their 'Odysseys' series, the Poetry Library's contribution to the 2018 London Literature Festival, and her work has been published in Britain's oldest and longest running literary periodical *The London Magazine*.

In 2020 the renowned US publisher Andrews McMeel published her collection *Tomorrow's Woman* alongside a collection of feminist poetry she edited titled *SMEAR*. This saw her work reach a global audience and in the same year her *Collected Poems* was translated into Spanish and published by Valparaíso Ediciones in Madrid. *The Financial Times* described *Tomorrow's Woman* as '*a beguiling, urgent, beautiful, lamenting, tender and powerful ode to the complexities of contemporary womanhood*' and Greta as a '*cultural Trojan horse*'.

Bellamacina is also an award-winning actor, screenwriter, and film director. Her debut feature film *Hurt By Paradise* was nominated for the prestigious *Michael Powell Award for Best British Feature Film* at the Edinburgh Film Festival, and for *Best UK Film* at Raindance. *The Evening Standard* wrote, '*Bellamacina is as precise and bold as Joanna Hogg.*'

Some of the poems in this book also appear in the film *Things and Other Things*, Greta's second collaboration with the renowned Italian avant-garde theatre director Riccardo Vannuccini, a sequel to their 2023 film *Commedia*.

CHEERIO

NEW
RIVER
PRESS
●